NO REGRETS

Finding the Right Path with a
Personal Finance Coach

A Common Sense Guide to *Achieving* and *Affording* Your Life Goals

BY
ROBERT ABBOUD
BEcon, CFP, PFP

No Regrets: A Common Sense Guide to *Achieving* and *Affording* Your Life Goals

Robert Abboud
Wealth Strategies
210 Centrum Blvd., Suite 209
Ottawa, ON K1E 3V7
rob@wealthstrategies.com

Published by Book Coach Press
Ottawa, Ontario, Canada
www.BookCoachPress.com
info@BookCoachPress.com

Printed and bound in Canada.

The advice and recommendations in this book are the opinions of the author and should in no way replace the services of a qualified financial planner. Care has been taken to appropriately reference any books or quotations used in the writing of this book. The author and publisher welcome any information enabling them to rectify any references or credit in subsequent editions.

Editors: Karen Lanouette, Brigitte Larocque, Heather Martin
Designer: Donald Lanouette
Printer: Quebecor

Library and Archives Canada Cataloguing in Publication
Abboud, Robert, 1968-
   No Regrets : A common sense guide to achieving and affording your life goals /
Robert Abboud.
Includes bibliographical references.

ISBN 0-9739071-6-9

    1. Finance, Personal. 2. Financial planners. 3. Investment advisors.

I. Title.

HG179.A22 2006   332.024   C2006-904758-8

Table of Contents

This book is dedicated to my wonderful wife
Brigitte and my incredible son Jeremy.
Jeremy, dream big, anything is possible.

FOREWORD

"Create a definite plan for carrying out your desire and begin at once, whether you are ready or not, to put this plan into action."
Napoleon Hill

In the busy and hectic world in which we live, it is easy to forget what is really important in life. All too often the focus is on money, making more, or spending more of it. It can be difficult to stop and take the time to determine what we want money to do for us as opposed to what we will do for money.

The measure of financial success should not be how much money we gather, but rather how well it is managed in order to fulfill our lives. In order to accomplish this, we need to determine what is important to us, identify our personal goals and most essential, put this in writing and create an action plan to help us attain these objectives. In the financial industry, the element of a properly crafted financial plan is so often non-existent. However, it is the most important tool to allow us to clearly see how we will achieve our goals. How will we know how well we are doing if we have no idea of where we are heading?

No Regrets is a common sense guide that shows you step by step how to determine what money means to you, how to set goals and then how to manage money wisely in order to achieve them. To maximize your results, the chapters dedicated to working with a Personal Finance Coach explain what to look for in a financial plan and what you should expect from your financial advisor/planner.

Through this simple, straightforward and motivational book, Robert Abboud brings you his no-nonsense approach to financial planning and reaching your life goals. He makes you stop and think about money in a way you may not have done before. The step-by-step explanations, the practical exercises and the 10-week action plan, make it easy to implement the recommendations. So read on and enjoy this refreshing approach to the life and financial planning process.

David Cork

David Cork is the best-selling author of The Pig and The Python, Bulls, Bears and Pigs and When the Pig Goes to Market.

Acknowledgements

Writing a book intended to help people reach their life and financial goals was a fantastic experience. There were many people who helped me with this project.

First, I want to thank my parents for always encouraging me to dream big and to go after my life goals. Special thanks to Diane Gaudet, who I have worked with for over eight years. Her help during the early edits of the book was much appreciated.

Phrasing many of my thoughts in an understandable manner was difficult at times. Thanks to my main editor, Heather Martin from Clarus Editing, for helping rephrase and simplify what I was trying to say.

A sincere thank you to my clients for sharing their life goals and dreams with me. It is truly an honour and a privilege to work with all of them.

I was honoured to have David Cork provide the foreword. He is an inspiration, both as an author of three bestsellers and as a colleague who is devoted to the financial planning process. Thank you again David.

Finally, thanks to my amazing wife Brigitte who kept encouraging me to finish this book. Her help with the editing, wording, formatting and title selection was priceless.

INTRODUCTION

"Don't buy things; buy freedom."
David Futrelle

Money: it's what everybody wants. But many of us don't feel we ever have enough, or are not really sure how to manage it if we do.

My first job out of university was at a bank. This allowed me to see firsthand how a range of people managed their money, from the Great Saver to the Great Borrower to the Great Worrier. Now I run my own financial planning practice, which focuses on helping families make the most of their money. Together, we discuss and plan for their hopes and dreams, their wish lists and travel plans. I find that this type of comprehensive planning is lacking in the financial services sector. This is what inspired me to write this book. I truly believe that we can all achieve many of our hopes and dreams, including a comfortable retirement; we just need to know how to do it. The answer doesn't lie in picking just the right stock or saving every dime at the expense of all pleasure. The answer is quite simple, all it takes is a little planning: **Life Goals Planning**.

A plan will allow you to achieve your goals while making the proper investments to get you there. Of course, we are all looking for the best possible investment return, but once we dig deeper and establish life and financial goals, we begin to realize that investments and rates of return are not the most important factors. For many investors, the suggestions that are made in the following pages may cause a fundamental shift in your way of thinking. The day-to-day fluctuations of investments are far less important than ultimately achieving one's life goals.

This should not imply that your investments are not important. It simply means they are just one of many aspects of your finances. They are the vehicles to help you meet your goals, plain and simple. If you take too much or too little risk, you are unlikely to reach financial independence and the freedom that goes with it. If you live beyond your means or, conversely, never spend a dime for pleasure, your dreams will remain similarly out of reach. If, however, your portfolio is tailored to your goals and needs while limiting unnecessary risk, you have a much greater chance of achieving the life you've always wanted.

One of the keys to understanding money is to remember that it is not all that matters in life. Money allows us certain privileges, freedoms and luxuries, but it can also provide a lot of stress and worry.

The most valuable asset that exists is time. We all get twenty-four hours in a day and only a certain amount of days until it's all over. How we allocate our time is far more important than how we allocate our investments. One thing that money does provide, however, is the option to pay someone else to do certain tasks so that we can spend time doing what we enjoy.

An example is changing the oil in our car. If we really wanted to, we could dedicate the time to jacking up the car and draining and refilling the oil. Then we would have to go to a waste management site to discard the used oil, not to mention cleaning up the spills in the garage. All of this would probably take at least one hour of our time (not to mention the frustration) and maybe save us $10 from the cost of driving to a garage and having them change the oil in fifteen minutes… and yes, you'll pay more for it, but you will gain a more valuable asset—and that's time.

In life, we have to determine what our priorities are and focus our allotted time accordingly. Nowadays, with the Internet and the overwhelming amount of available information, you can do almost anything online as long as you have the time and the patience needed. You can register a company, build your own website, do your taxes, diagnose your own illness…the list goes on. Or you could save the hours that it would take and pay someone to handle it. Seeing as they do it for a living, they will probably do a much better job.

Throughout the book you will see that I always recommend and suggest that one seek and pay for the services of a Personal Finance Coach (a certain type of Financial Planner/Advisor). I truly believe that most people do not have enough time or energy to properly take care of their own finances and that we need a professional to help us. Leaving our finances unattended leads to unnecessary stresses. Just as you would hire a dentist to help you with your teeth, you should hire a professional to help you with your finances.

The first step to **Life Goals Planning** is to evaluate your goals in life. Which do you feel you most want to achieve? Throughout my years in the financial services industry, I have seen too many people who have far too much money and yet have many unfulfilled wishes and dreams. The magic of **Life Goals Planning** is that it allows you to set goals for your life that really matter to you.

For example, my wife Brigitte and I went through the exercise of writing down all the goals that we wish to accomplish during our lives. They ranged from travel destinations, raising a family, learning to fly, to charitable causes—activities we felt would bring meaning and happiness to our lives. None of these included having the best asset allocation possible or paying the lowest management fee on our investments. We also wrote down some financial goals, such as retiring at a certain age with a level of income that will allow us to have the retirement lifestyle we envision for ourselves.

Many of the life goals we have require money to bring to fruition. This is where **Life Goals Planning** comes in. Once you establish your life and financial goals, you can then work on determining 1) whether they are realistic, based on your current circumstances, and 2) how to reach these goals. We'll discuss this in more detail in Chapter 2, Setting and Achieving Goals.

This book is meant to help readers focus on the important elements in life, and, through proper financial planning and **Life Goals Planning**, achieve these objectives.

One of the saddest things I saw while working at the bank was elderly clients who had an overabundance of money, yet whose biggest concern was getting an extra .25% on a GIC (Guaranteed Investment Certificate). They would not indulge and buy themselves so much as a new hat. Many of these clients were widows who would share with me all the regrets they had about life and how they wished they had done this or that while their spouse was still alive. The most common phrase I heard was, "My spouse always wanted to (fill in the blank) but he never got around to doing it."

There is, of course, the other extreme, where people pay no attention to their financial affairs and pile up debts to build a house of cards that is always one gust of air away from falling apart. And believe me, it always does fall apart.

From my experience, these are the **5 Biggest Mistakes People Make With Money**:

1. They don't have a clear idea of what they want to achieve with their money.

Until you set some concrete goals and objectives, how would you know what to do with your money? Once goals are set, then you can focus your thoughts and actions towards achieving these.

2. They do not have control over their monthly cashflow.

Too many people live month-to-month, are not aware of where their money goes, and feel like they are never getting ahead. A business would never consider working without a budget. Would you invest in a company that didn't track their income and expenses?

3. They delay making financial decisions.

Procrastination can be one of the greatest obstacles to reaching an objective. Many people wait for just the right time or suffer paralysis through over-analysis and never make a decision.

4. They have no formal plan for achieving their financial goals.

Many people spend more time planning their annual holiday then they do their financial future. It is very difficult to reach a financial goal if you do not have a plan that illustrates the steps on how to get there.

5. They don't seek professional advice on their whole financial picture.

Most people have their financial life scattered in different areas. They hold their pension with their employer, purchase life insurance through an insurance salesperson and stocks through a stockbroker, and they deposit their savings in a bank account. They don't have anyone analyzing the whole picture and creating a comprehensive financial plan taking into consideration their financial objectives and current situation. This is where a Personal Finance Coach can optimize results by taking a look at their total financial picture.

This book will provide the advice needed to avoid these mistakes.

Prudent financial management, the assistance of a Personal Finance Coach (PFC) and allowing yourself to make the most of your money will permit you to enjoy both a happy, fulfilled life and a comfortable retirement. Read on, and best of luck with your **Life Goals Planning** adventure!

CHAPTER
1

What Does Money Mean to You?

> *"Without the rich heart,*
> *wealth is an ugly beggar."*
> Ralph Waldo Emerson

Beginning Your Life Goals Plan

The first step in determining your **Life Goals Plan** is to figure out what money means to you. When you think of money, what comes to mind? Do you always want more money? And if so, why, or what for? Does it give you a feeling of security? Or is it to buy all the latest gadgets? Or to provide a legacy for your family? Or a comfortable retirement for yourself? Does money scare or confuse you?

Money means different things to different people. Some visualize changing the world with it; others would be content with a new couch. What's important is what *you* plan to do with your money. This is the first step in building a practical plan to achieve your dreams. Think about what you do with your money now.

- Do you spend everything you earn?
- Do you save regularly?
- Do you spend it on travel?
- Do you give it to charity?
- Do you have more than you know what to do with?
- Do you live beyond your means and find it necessary to borrow?
- Do you even know where your money goes?

Regardless of what you currently do with your money, chances are that you've never thought extensively about what it represents to you. What I've found is that money almost always translates into a very human need for security, comfort, and family. Beyond these basic needs, it can mean freedom to do what you want with your life, and the ability to make a difference in the lives of others.

The Hierarchy of Human Needs

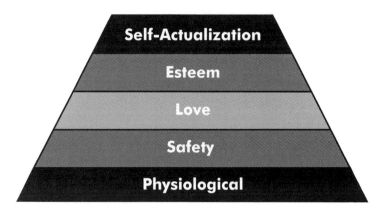

A psychologist named Abraham Maslow developed a hierarchy of human needs (Maslow, 1943). Maslow studied exemplary people such as Albert Einstein, Jane

Addams, Eleanor Roosevelt, and Thomas Jefferson to complete his landmark study. His theory contends that as human beings meet "basic needs," they seek to satisfy successively "higher needs" that occupy a set hierarchy.

Physiological Needs

Physiological needs are the very basic needs such as air, water, food, and sleep. Once these needs are met, we begin to think of other needs.

Safety Needs

Safety needs have to do with establishing stability and consistency. These needs are mostly psychological in nature. We need the safety of a home and other things. Once these needs are met, the next stage begins.

Love Needs

Love and belonging are next on the ladder. Human beings have a desire to belong to clubs, work groups, religious groups, and family. We need to feel loved by others, to be accepted by others. We need to be needed.

Esteem Needs

Self-esteem results from competence or mastery of a task. If we really wish to master a task or achieve a goal, we need to have the freedom to do so.

Self-Actualization

The need for self-actualization is the need to become everything that one is capable of becoming. People who have everything can maximize their potential. They are able to help others. They can seek knowledge, peace and self-fulfillment.

As we move up to the top of the hierarchy of needs, we begin to place a greater value on non-monetary things, such as helping others and becoming more spiritual.

Life Goals Planning Hierarchy

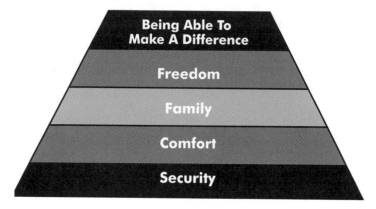

When you think about it, most of these human needs are directly tied to money and life goals, and to what money means to us. Let's look at each of these needs in further detail through the Life Goals Planning Hierarchy.

Money Means Security

The primary concern is to have enough money to cover the basic living necessities.

Once this is taken care of, the biggest concern most people have is whether they will have enough money to retire comfortably. Once you have a plan developed and you know that, based on certain assumptions, you should have sufficient savings to allow you to retire, you may find that you let out a huge sigh of relief. Don't underestimate the feeling of security of knowing that your retirement future is looked after.

Another area related to security is the knowledge that if something unexpected should happen, the individual's family will have enough money to uphold the lifestyle they wish for or have become accustomed to.

Many people need the security of knowing that there is an emergency fund set aside in case of sudden contingencies such as being laid off, unexpected home repairs, health issues or any other type of emergency. Just having this money set aside as a safety net provides a level of security that many individuals describe as very reassuring and peaceful.

Money Means Comfort

Money provides comfort to all of us. We all have varying concepts of what comfort means to us, how much comfort we desire, and how much money is needed to provide that comfort. For many of us, comfort means having a nicely furnished home, a car and a nice garden. Money can provide the comfort for which we have always hoped. The feeling of having achieved the life goal of owning a home and having certain luxuries is very rewarding and comforting. The feeling of walking into the kind of home you have always imagined and then easing into your favourite reading chair by the fireplace can be priceless.

Money Means Family

The truth, unfortunate as it may be, is that nowadays, it is practically impossible to raise a family without sufficient income. And, of course, the larger the family, the larger the income needed. If you ask people how many children they would like to have, most would say two. If you then ask: "If money weren't an issue, how many children would you like to have?" surprisingly, many people say three or more. Money also allows us the opportunity to take care of our loved ones. It enables us to provide a comfortable home and lifestyle, and to ensure a proper education for them.

If you are single and looking to meet someone and start a family, more often than not, potential spouses want to ensure that you have the ability to provide for the family. If you don't believe me, ask any single, thirty plus person what they are looking for in a potential mate. The answer is usually: a nice person who is gainfully employed and financially comfortable. Not many people are lining up to enter into a relationship that will burden them with a truckload of debt and dependency.

Money Means Freedom

The more money we possess, the more freedom we have to do certain activities and to achieve certain life goals. When we are in our early working years, we are usually busy building our lives by purchasing furniture, a car, clothes, a stereo, a television, appliances, etc. Most of the time we have to borrow money to allow us to enjoy the lifestyle we desire today, as we plan to pay for it tomorrow—or, more likely, in three to five years. At this period in our lives, we usually do not have excess money (or even know the *meaning* of excess money).

As we move along in our lives, our salaries begin to increase. Maybe we meet and live with a significant other. At this point, our cost of living may come down, since we have two incomes to provide for many fixed expenses that we paid for as an individual before. This increase in monetary resources may allow us the freedom to start thinking about getting married, having children, or taking an annual holiday.

In the next phase of our lives, we are typically in our high earning years, and have little or no debt. We usually have a lot more extra income that we can spend however we wish. This may give us the freedom to reduce our workweek and to spend more time doing what we love, be it golfing, fishing, or enjoying the company of our loved ones.

Money Means Being Able to Make a Difference

Once we have satisfied our other human needs, we can then turn our attention to making a difference in the world. This is the pinnacle of achieving one's life and financial goals. Once at this stage in life we can do anything we wish. We may want to share our wealth with the less fortunate. We can increase our knowledge by taking time to study a topic that has always fascinated us. We can focus on our spiritual side by delving deeper into the meaning of life. Maybe that means a pilgrimage to Mecca or a retreat to the Vatican for some spiritual renewal, or a trek to Tibet or India for a journey of enlightenment. Each individual defines this differently, and there are many ways to follow this path.

At this stage you begin to ask questions like "Why am I here?" and "How can I make a difference?" You begin to place less value on monetary issues, and more on non-monetary ones.

Warren Buffett, one of the greatest investors of all time and the second-richest person in North America, announced in July of 2006 that he will begin giving away 85% of his $44 billion fortune to five philanthropic foundations (Loomis, 2006). He has reached the pinnacle of self-actualization. Often referred to as "The Oracle of Omaha," he will certainly leave a lasting legacy and may affect the lives of millions of people. Bill Gates, the founder of Microsoft and the wealthiest man in North America, donates hundreds of millions to worthwhile causes each year. For these and other individuals, it is no longer about money. They strive to succeed for other reasons, such as self-fulfillment, the mental challenge and making a difference in the world.

Determining What Money Means to You

Think long and hard about what you would like your money to do for you at various stages in your life: next year, five years down the road, in ten years, or when you retire. Do you envision owning a new car or home? Do you dream of sending your children to university? Have you always wanted to start your own business? Would you like to volunteer abroad?

Chapter Two will provide some solid principles for prioritizing your list of dreams and making them, or at least some of them, a reality. For now, the practicality of your dreams and goals is beside the point. What is essential is that these objectives speak to you. Determine what your money means to you and for what purpose you want to use it. This simple first step is fundamental to your future success.

Chapter Summary

Beginning Your Life Goals Plan

Think about what you do with your money now and what you would ultimately like to do with it.

The Life Goals Planning Hierarchy of Human Needs

The Life Goals Planning hierarchy defines our money needs as beginning with the basic needs of security, comfort, and family, and progressing to freedom and the ability to make a difference. Use this paradigm as a framework to envision where you would like your money to take you.

Money Means Security

The knowledge that you will be able to retire comfortably, that your family is cared for in the event that something happens to you, or that you have a safety net in case of emergency offers a sense of security that will allow you to enjoy your life and think about other things.

Money Means Comfort

Money can allow us certain comforts and luxuries that enrich our lives and make day-to-day living more pleasurable.

Money Means Family

Most of us would like to have a family, and it takes a certain amount of money to achieve this goal. If you have a family already, you want the best for them. Money can't buy you love, but it does make your family prospects more viable.

Money Means Freedom

Money provides the freedom and the means by which you can achieve many of your dreams.

Money Means Being Able to Make a Difference

Having reached the pinnacle of achieving one's life and financial goals, you can now turn to helping others or following a spiritual path of your own.

Determining What Money Means to You

Think long and hard about where you see yourself in the coming years. What would you like your money to do for you?

CHAPTER
2

Setting and Achieving Goals

*"Whatever the mind can conceive and believe,
the mind can achieve."*
Napoleon Hill

Getting Started

One of the keys to successful **Life Goals Planning** is clearly defining your goals and then setting forth a plan to achieve them. Everybody has goals, but the most successful people in the world actually achieve them by writing them down and then creating a strategy or plan for reaching them.

Goal planning for individuals should be very similar to goal planning for a business. Any successful, well-run business works with a business plan that sets targets to be achieved by a certain date. If a business simply stated that it wanted to increase sales by 50% but had no plan to realize this goal, the chances of achieving it would be slim to none.

Unfortunately, most individuals do not think like businesses, and therefore never create a plan based on their life goals, let alone write their goals down.

Your Life Goals

The first step to setting and achieving goals is to think about all the things you want to do in your lifetime, and set them down on paper. There is an incredible power in writing down a thought, an idea, or a goal. It makes what's in your head a potential reality. Can you imagine if Edison had never put his thoughts on the development of a practical, incandescent electric light (the light bulb) on paper and then tried and tried until he got it right? He took a thought, converted it to paper, and then built an action plan to make it a reality. So grab a piece of paper and draw a line down the centre. If you are married or have a significant other, I suggest you sit together and set down your goals on separate sheets of paper but share and compare your goals as you go along.

On the left-hand side of the paper write Life Goals at the top. Now start listing all the goals you have for yourself. Think hard and list even the smallest, most trivial ones; they can be some of the easiest and most rewarding goals to achieve. Think of travel destinations you wish to visit, activities you want to do, talents you want to cultivate, books you want to read, or things you want to learn. Once these life goals are established, share them with your spouse and see if you get any good ideas from each other. It's also interesting to note how many you do or do not have in common!

Setting Life Goals

Life Goals
Have 2 children
Visit Europe for 3 weeks
Lose 20 pounds
Milk a cow
Run a marathon
Learn to play guitar
Read 5 books a year
Visit China for 5 weeks
Buy a Harley Davidson

Your Financial Goals

Take a second piece of paper, put a line down the middle, and on the left-hand side write Financial Goals at the top. List some of your financial goals, such as when you would like to retire, what your goal is vis-à-vis your family's well-being should you become ill or pass away, and what type of legacy (if any) you wish to leave to the next generation. You'll find that your Financial Goals list will be significantly shorter than your Life Goals list. Most people have only a few financial goals, the most important being: I want to retire at age ___ and provide a comfortable lifestyle for the rest of my own life as well as my spouse's.

Another goal that is usually mentioned is paying off the mortgage. This is a big milestone for most people, and represents the moment when they'll be able to shift a large part of their income to other things. Consider also whether you wish to save for your children's higher education. Be as thorough as possible with this list: even though it may not be as much fun to think about as your life goals, it is a practical stepping-stone to achieving them.

Setting Financial Goals

Financial Goals

Retire at age 55
Pay off mortgage
Save for children's education
Ensure family is cared for
if I die

The Cost Equation

What about that right-hand side of those sheets? Write Cost and Projected Year at the top right of each of your goal sheets.

Now comes the hard part. You need to prioritize each of your life and financial goals based on your desire to achieve them, their affordability, and your realistic chances of attaining them.

Let's start with your life goals. Review all your goals and try to prioritize them by which ones you really want to accomplish. Place them in order of precedence, and then put an approximate dollar value on what it will cost for you to complete each goal. Let's say, for example, your top three goals are: spend three weeks backpacking through Europe, learn to play the guitar and milk a cow. You need to place an approximate cost on each item. Travelling through Europe may cost $3,000 to $10,000 depending on the comfort you need and activities planned. Determine a ballpark figure for how much it would cost; let's say $5,000. Then do the same for the guitar goal. Let's estimate the cost of guitar lessons at $800. (If you are really bad with music, add an extra $500; I know I'd need to). The goal of milking a cow may not have a cost associated with it—except for the time needed to find out where to go to milk a cow!

Costing & Projecting Life Goals

Life Goals	Cost & Projected Year	
Visit Europe for 3 weeks	$5,000	2011
Milk a cow	$0	2010
Learn to play guitar	$1,300	2012

Putting a dollar figure on your life goals is crucial. If you don't put these types of goals in writing and cost them out, how will you know if they are affordable or achievable?

Costing & Projecting Financial Goals

Financial Goals	Cost & Projected Year	
Retire at age 55	?	2021
Pay off mortgage	?	2016
Save for children's education	?	2016
Ensure family is cared for if I die	?	Now

You'll notice that for all the financial goals, the space for cost is blank. This is because costing financial goals requires complex calculations based on certain assumptions and forecasts. To determine, for example, your retirement objective, you might surf the Internet, research a reasonable after-tax retirement income expectation, have it increase with inflation, and also use a realistic rate of return in your calculations. Then you'll need to determine how your existing pension and government pension will affect your calculations. Factor in taxation rates to establish the ultimate amount of savings required to retire. Then determine how much you have to save annually or monthly.

You can go through that long process, or you can consult with your financial planner, who is educated and trained to do it for you. Yes, there is a cost involved in seeing a financial planner, but it is a minor amount to pay for the value you will receive and the impact it will have on the rest of your life.

Timelines

OK, so you've set several life and financial goals, made sure you have put them in order, and placed a dollar value on each one. Once you know how much you need to save in order to achieve your financial goals, then you can figure out what to do with the remaining cashflow. This excess cashflow is what dreams are built on. It is this excess that you can redirect towards fulfilling the Europe dream or buying the new furniture or taking a trip next year with the family.

Now, write a year next to each goal. This will help you visualize each one, and when you would like to achieve it. Depending on finances and the scope of your dreams, you may decide that you would like to achieve three fulfilling activities every year, or you may start a tradition in which you accomplish one dream every year. Once it's all set down on paper and you have a fairly realistic picture of where you're headed and what you'll be able to achieve, you and your spouse can create a short and long-range schedule that will allow you to realize much more than you thought possible.

Accomplishing the Dream

One of the main reasons people do not achieve their goals is that they don't take the time to write them down and create an action plan. It's difficult to express how rewarding it is to sit with clients, review their goals, and then, when affordable, work these into their financial plan. This allows them to see that the goal is definitely achievable, and that they will meet the goal by a certain year as long as they set aside x amount of dollars each month. We have clients who are saving for a Harley Davidson in ten years, a trip to Europe in two years, a cruise to Alaska in three years, and a tax-free estate for their grandchildren. This is one of the most rewarding parts of my job. The whole idea of financial planning is that it should allow you to maximize the value of your dollars and achieve all your life goals and dreams.

It's important to note that until you run the calculations as to whether you can afford these, you will not know if they are achievable or realistic, given your income, health, and other factors.

Before I left the bank to start my own financial planning practice, the idea of starting my own firm was simply a dream. It was always on my mind that I would one day set up my own practice, and help families attain their financial and life goals. Well, all it took was for a client to ask me one day why I had not yet gone out on my own as a financial planner. The minute he uttered the words, I realized this had to become a reality for me. Immediately after he left, I wrote down my goal of setting up my own financial planning practice, when I wanted to achieve this goal, and how much it would cost.

That night I began to put all the pieces of the plan, my plan, together. As the plan set out, within six months, I had rented office space, handed in my resignation, and done all the securities paperwork required by the Ontario Securities Commission. My financial planning practice, Wealth Strategies, opened in September of 1996 (one month ahead of target).

Looking back now, all of this may never have occurred had my client not jolted me into moving that goal from my head to paper. To this day, I am still in touch with this client and extremely grateful for that meeting years ago.

Writing this book is another item on my list of life goals. So, if you are reading this, it means that the book has been published and I have checked off another goal from the list!

Remember, if you don't set your goals down in writing, it is much harder to achieve them. As well, if you are working with a planner, you need to share your goals so that they can work with you to achieve them. Now it's your turn, so dream big!

Chapter Summary

Getting Started

Think about your goals as you would a business plan. Write them down and create a strategy to achieve them.

Your Life Goals

What would you like to accomplish in your lifetime? List everything from the trivial to your wildest dreams.

Your Financial Goals

Do you dream of living mortgage-free? Retiring at age fifty-five? Contributing to your children's education? Be specific.

The Cost Equation

Prioritize your life and financial goals based on your desire to achieve them, their affordability, and your realistic chances of attaining them.

Timelines

Create a schedule in order to visualize and prioritize your goals.

Accomplishing the Dream

Take your life and financial goals to a qualified financial planner, who will help you create an action plan that will turn your dreams into a reality.

CHAPTER
3

Plan for the Future, Live for Today

"Never spend your money before you have it."
Thomas Jefferson

Appearances Are Deceiving –'All Hat, No Cattle'

One of the most difficult things to achieve is to successfully plan for the future while enjoying today. Sure, there are lots of people who are really enjoying the present. They have expensive cars, boats, cottages, beautiful furniture, big homes, and the best of everything. Unfortunately, in most cases they also have one other thing that you can't see as clearly as the BMW and Mercedes in the driveway: it's called debt. And in keeping with all their other possessions, it's usually very, very big. Many people forgo a realistic lifestyle simply to keep up with the Joneses. If the neighbour just got a new SUV, maybe we should get one as well. If your friends just installed an in-ground pool, we might really need one, too. This kind of thinking might sound silly on paper, but all too often in a world of abundance, real life has a way of blurring the line between "want" and "need"—and nothing looks so good as your friend's latest toy.

Many people may not be aware that most millionaires are everyday people who work 9 to 5 jobs, shop at discount stores like Wal-Mart, and drive simple, reliable and, in most cases, used cars. The majority of millionaires have created their wealth by watching how they spend their money and never buying beyond their means. In a landmark study and book, The Millionaire Next Door (1996), authors Thomas J. Stanley and William D. Danko make a clear distinction between the truly wealthy and those that spend a lot of money to look wealthy. They determined that most millionaires live below their means and believe that financial independence is more important than displaying social status. As well, they noted that most millionaires ran a very tight budget and were aware of all their expenses over the previous year.

There are no get-rich-quick schemes that truly work. There is, however, one slow process that does work, and it is this: work hard, invest wisely, watch how you spend your money, and never buy more than you can afford.

Some people may have the impression that millionaires drive luxury cars and eat caviar all day. The reality is quite different. Many people driving around in luxury cars have luxurious debts that you never hear about. Remember, most of the time, people only want to share the good news about their finances. How many people have you heard bragging about how much debt they have or how they lost 90% of their investments in Nortel (a technology stock)? A large part of the population did lose lots of money investing in Nortel, but nobody brags about that kind of thing.

Focusing on the Goal

The objective here is to stay focused on your personal goals and ignore all the noise. This way, you can focus on the goals you have set, instead of somebody else's vision of what your life should look like. It is this clarity that gives **Life Goals Planning** its value.

It is important to understand the underlying principle of planning for the future but living for today. We all want to enjoy our lives, but we also want to have the comfort of knowing that we will have a secure (and, perhaps, even an early) retirement. The trick is balancing these two desires in the real world, and that's where financial planning comes in. The exercise of putting your finances down on paper and weighing your expenses versus what is left over gives you options you may not know existed. You have finite resources that can provide pleasure and comfort either now, in the near future, or in the more distant future. Having a detailed list of your life and financial goals, and their costs as compared with your income, goes a long way towards helping you make an educated decision.

Assume you were at your friend Larry's house last night and he took you to the marina where you were really taken by his sailboat and you thought "I can see myself sailing on a boat like that. I need a sailboat, too." Let's assume the cost of a comparable (or slightly better) sailboat is $15,000. The good news is you have set aside $15,000 that you were going to use to make a contribution to your retirement fund. Because according to your plan, you need to set aside a minimum of $15,000 per year to allow you to achieve your goal of retiring at age fifty-five. So a dilemma ensues: Do you buy the boat with the $15,000 (and blow Larry's socks off) or do you invest in your retirement? The choice is up to you, but you should know the consequences so that you can make an educated decision.

Let's say you call your financial planner and they crunch the numbers for you and advise you that, if you decide not to invest in your retirement fund, it means you can no longer retire at age fifty-five. You will now have to work two extra years before you can afford to retire (taking into consideration lost compound growth of the would-be investment). With that information, and a deep discussion with your significant other, you can determine whether it's worth two additional years of working to buy a boat today.

Budget is a Good Word

For every financial action you take, there are financial repercussions—period. We all have a limited amount of money to allow us to live. You need to ensure that you make the most of this, and that you understand how money grows and compounds when you invest it for the future. $15,000 today may grow to $70,000 in twenty years or $200,000 in thirty years, depending on how it is managed. Before you can plan for the future, you need to complete the exercises in the previous chapter, which will determine what your goals are and how much it will cost to achieve them. Then you need to complete a cashflow analysis (budget) to see what is affordable. So let's assume a household earns $5,200 per month after tax and it costs them $4,000 per month to live, including rent/mortgage, utilities, property taxes, food, spending money, miscellaneous expenses, etc. (see sample cashflow analysis/budget on following page).

That leaves $1,200 per month of surplus cashflow. Now they may not think they have this surplus because at the end of each month, there is little or nothing left. This is common. What usually happens is that we spend what we earn, regardless of our expenses. However, if we pay ourselves first, i.e., automatically set the money aside towards our goals, then we should run a balanced budget. Once you set up a proper budget (cashflow strategy, more on this in Chapter 5, Getting the Most from Your Money), it will allow you to enjoy life and save for your goals.

Let's go back to the scenario of the family with $1,200 of surplus assets. They had decided that priority #1 was to retire at age fifty-five, and through financial forecasts,

Sample Cashflow Analysis/Budget

	Existing		Revised		Notes
Pension Income (Net)					
Salary (Net)	$3,000.00	58%	$3,000.00	58%	
Spouse's Salary (Net)	$2,200.00	42%	$2,200.00	42%	
Other					
Monthly Net Income:	$5,200.00	100%	$5,200.00	100%	
Less:					
Mortgage/Rent	$800.00	15%	$800.00	15%	
House Insurance	$50.00	1%	$50.00	1%	
Property Taxes	$200.00	4%	$200.00	4%	
Car Loan	$200.00	4%	$200.00	4%	
Car Insurance	$150.00	3%	$150.00	3%	
Car Maintenance	$50.00	1%	$50.00	1%	
Pocket Money	$200.00	4%	$200.00	4%	
Other Loan	$0.00	0%	$0.00	0%	
Memberships	$0.00	0%	$0.00	0%	
Credit Card	$0.00	0%	$0.00	0%	
Groceries	$600.00	12%	$600.00	12%	
Utilities (cable, heat, hydro, phone, water)	$450.00	9%	$450.00	9%	
Clothing	$300.00	6%	$300.00	6%	
Entertainment	$200.00	4%	$200.00	4%	
Gifts	$200.00	4%	$200.00	4%	
Education Savings	$0.00	0%	$0.00	0%	
Other	$0.00	0%	$0	0%	
Gas (automobile)	$200.00	4%	$200.00	4%	
Life Insurance	$50.00	1%	$50.00	1%	
House Maintenance	$100.00	2%	$100.00	2%	
Medical	$0.00	0%	$0.00	0%	
Charity	$50.00	1%	$50.00	1%	
Child Care	$0.00	0%	$0.00	0%	
Miscellaneous	$200.00	4%	$200.00	4%	
Goal #1 - RRSP Savings	$0.00	0%	$600.00	12%	SET UP MONTHLY SAVINGS PLAN
Goal #2 - Pay off mortgage in 10 years	$0.00	0%	$150.00	3%	INCREASE MONTHLY PAYMENTS
Goal #3 - Travel	$0.00	0%	$250.00	5%	SET UP MONTHLY SAVINGS PLAN
Goal #4 - Harley Davidson	$0.00	0%	$200.00	4%	SET UP MONTHLY SAVINGS PLAN
Other Savings	$0.00	0%	$0.00	0%	
Total Expenses:	$4,000.00	77%	$5,200.00	100%	
Surplus / Shortfall	$1,200.00	23%			

determined that, in order to do this with a retirement income to meet their needs, they must save $7,200 per year, or $600 per month. The first thing they should do is set up an automatic withdrawal from their bank account directly into their RRSP. This fulfills goal #1.

If goal #2 is to pay off the mortgage in ten years, and this involves an additional $150 per month, then they would have that amount redirected to the mortgage automatically each month.

If goal #3 is to travel annually, and the cost is $3,000 per year, they would then set up an automatic transfer of $250 per month to a high-yield savings account. This leaves $200 per month.

Let's assume goal #4 is to buy a Harley Davidson in fifteen years and to ride across Canada. The anticipated cost is $40,000. They would set up an automatic transfer of $200 per month to a high-yield savings account. After fifteen years there would be approximately $36,000 saved up for this goal. Not quite enough, but now the dream Harley and trip, once thought to be impossible, are within reach. If this couple decides to buy a less expensive Harley or wait another twenty months, another dream or goal will be fulfilled.

Automate for Success

As I mentioned earlier, my wife and I have listed our life and financial goals. We also have automatic monthly withdrawals made to allow us to achieve these goals. Some of the money is for our future retirement and therefore invested for the long term in applicable long-term investments. Other portions are for short-term goals such as annual travel and home renovations. These are directed to high-yield bank accounts. It is key that you direct your monies to the appropriate investment vehicle. If you know you will need your money in less than five years, no risk should be taken. Make sure that you invest in a non-fluctuating asset such as a high-yield bank account, term deposit, or a money market fund.

We all have very busy lives, and anything that can simplify our lives should be embraced. Automating most or all of your financial transactions can save you significant time and hassle and help ensure that you reach your life and financial goals. You are probably aware that most household bills can be paid automatically from your bank account. You still receive your bill in advance and are informed of the amount owed, but the company simply takes the payment automatically from your bank account when it is due. It is a simple and effective system that saves you time. Basically someone else is doing the work for you.

This same type of automation applies to your goals, and helps you discipline yourself to save towards them. Most of our clients are set up on automatic savings plans for various goals, such as retirement in eight years, education savings for the kids, a trip to Cuba, a '66 Mustang convertible, or a cottage by the lake. They always say they are amazed at how quickly the monthly savings add up. They never knew they would be able to save these amounts, as they were spending everything they earned each month. Remember, if an amount is earmarked for something specific and is automatically set aside, it doesn't end up being spent. After a couple of months, most say they don't miss the amount taken out each month. It's as if it never existed.

We recently did a comparison of net worth for one couple from when we met them in 1999, compared to today, 2006. Their net worth had more than doubled in seven years. You will be amazed at how easy and painless (not to mention rewarding) forced savings can be. David Chilton, author of the best selling *The Wealthy Barber*, was one of the first people to popularize paying yourself first. His book sold millions of copies and helped numerous people become wealthier with a simple, common sense solution to saving.

Plan for your future and live for today by taking a look at your monthly expenses, budgeting what you'll need to meet your short and long-term goals, and automating those withdrawals so that you don't have to think about them. In order to get the most from your money, ask the advice of a financial planner/advisor when setting up this system. Instead of spending your time constantly juggling finances and wondering if you'll ever get out of debt or have enough for retirement, you can enjoy the peace of mind of knowing that each day brings you one step closer to your dreams.

Chapter Summary

Appearances are Deceiving

Don't be misled by the elaborate lifestyles of others. Focus instead on what you can afford.

___

Focusing on the Goal

Keep your objectives in mind and ignore the noise. Determine what's important to you and how you will use your finite resources to achieve it.

___

Budget is a Good Word

Itemize your expenses and prioritize what you would like to do with the surplus.

___

Automate for Success

Direct your money towards funding your goals by automatically debiting your account.

___

CHAPTER
4

Your Roadmap to the Future

*"If you don't know where you are going,
any road will take you there."*

Chinese proverb

Your Financial Plan

Since 1991, I have worked in the financial services industry and I have seen many different individuals, ranging from the forty-five-year-old millionaire to the sixty-eight-year-old retiree who is living below the poverty line. The question I kept asking myself was what makes these two people so very different? I came up with what I feel is the answer: planning. Having a plan is the key to a financially successful retirement and reaching one's life goals. You hear it over and over again, but nobody seems to pay attention. I find it unbelievable that so many people say they have no time to take care of their finances, but they do have ten to twenty hours a week to spend in front of the television or on the Internet.

I'm sure you have heard this before, "If you fail to plan, you plan to fail." Why is it that the majority of people do not have a financial plan? A game plan is common practice in any sport, as is a business plan in the working world. Even a vacation requires a travel plan, an itinerary that lists the things you'd like to do while you're there, in the time you have available. So why is it that some people drift through life with no clear idea of their finances, or how long those finances will last? There are two likely reasons: the intimidation factor, and an "I'll get around to it eventually" attitude.

Let's talk about the intimidation factor first. Many people aren't comfortable with managing money, and that's OK, as long as they hire someone who is. One thing I want to make sure you understand is how important it is to work with a financial planner/advisor. By this, I don't mean someone who takes your cheque and invests it; that is an investment salesperson. I'm talking about somebody who assesses *your* overall picture, is aware of all your assets, liabilities and expenses, not only your investments, then sets up a plan for you, and helps you follow through on it. Somebody who cares about your well-being and becomes a trusted family advisor, your Personal Finance Coach (PFC) (more on choosing a PFC in Chapter 6, Why You Need a Personal Finance Coach).

As for the procrastinators, it only stands to reason that the sooner you create a plan, the more money you will accumulate, and the better off you will be down the road.

Saving money, becoming wealthy and achieving your goals is not an impossible dream. And you are the one who will benefit from this effort. If you begin to plan and save now, I am confident you can do it.

A Map to the Future

When travelling by car to unfamiliar territory, it is essential to have a map with you to help guide you. If you want to get to Florida, you know that you could hop in the car and head south and eventually get there. Or you could buy a map, take the most direct route, and get there in less time and with less stress. Financial planning is the same idea. It provides the map to get you to retirement and to meet your other life goals. We all know we need to save for retirement, but how much, and how do we invest it? How many times have you retired in your life? This is unfamiliar territory. You need a map and a guide to help take you there.

Many people are not aware of what a financial plan is or what areas it should cover. Here are **the basics of what a financial plan should cover**:

Executive Summary of the Plan

This is a summary that highlights each section of your plan and points out recommended strategies to implement it. Your executive summary is meant to assist you in visualizing what you need to do to accomplish your goals.

Net Worth

This gives you a snapshot of where you are at today. Net worth is calculated by subtracting your liabilities from your assets. The result is your net worth. This should be used as a yardstick to measure your progress as the years pass. Remember: if you reduce debt or increase savings, your net worth will increase.

Retirement Planning

This section determines how much you need to save annually to meet your retirement goals. For example, you may wish to retire at fifty-five with an annual after-tax income of $42,000 in today's dollars. What does that mean? How much would you have to put aside each year or month to achieve this goal? What rate of return is realistic? What will happen if your investments earn more—or less? These are important factors of which to be aware.

The other important piece of information that retirement planning will help you determine is your required rate of return. Many people believe that they need to earn as much as possible on their investments and sometimes forget about the risk that is associated with more aggressive types of investments. A financial plan will tell you what your personal rate of return needs to be to allow you to achieve your goal. This personal rate of return then determines how much risk must be taken in creating your portfolio.

Assume that two individuals aged forty-five have similar retirement lifestyle needs, i.e., a wish to retire at age fifty-five. They need about $42,000 per year of after-tax income in retirement, plus $10,000 per year for travel until age seventy-five. Investor A has a $50,000 pension at age fifty-five and investments of $3 million, while investor B has no pension and $300,000 of investments. As you can imagine, investor A does not need to take on as much risk as Investor B. Reasonable rates of return that will ensure a higher probability of achieving your objective vary from 4% to 8%.

Portfolio Recommendations

This is where an asset allocation model is prepared for you to advise you on how much you should invest in the various types of investments such as growth, income or alternative investments, and of that, how much should be invested in Canadian or international investments, etc. This asset allocation works off the previous calculation of what your personal rate of return needs to be. It is important that you understand the portfolio recommendations. Remember, you own the portfolio, so you should understand the volatility associated with it. You should be comfortable with the recommendations made and should have an idea of the level of risk involved in your recommended portfolio.

Tax Planning

This section identifies tax saving opportunities, such as making spousal contributions, holding capital gains and dividend bearing investments in non-registered accounts and holding interest bearing investments in registered accounts. Tax planning can include tax sheltering, income-splitting strategies, and many other recommendations. Your planner will usually find sufficient tax savings to more than cover the cost of preparing the financial plan.

Insurance Planning

This section covers the need for proper insurance coverage for replacement of income in case of death, disability, or critical illness. There are many types of insurance; each one will be beneficial for some people and not for others. I find it surprising that so many people are underinsured or not insured at all. If you do not set up the proper insurance coverage to deal with potential catastrophe, you may leave your family not just suffering the loss of a loved one, but also with a huge concern: how will they replace lost income so that they can continue to live the lifestyle you worked so hard to achieve?

Estate Planning

This area covers the need for, and makes recommendations regarding, Wills, Power of Attorneys, Guardianship, and Testamentary Trusts. As well, it discusses multi-generational giving and tax-free inheritances. In most cases planners can make recommendations that will save the estate thousands of dollars, allowing more to go to the desired beneficiaries and not to the government.

I am always surprised that so few people take the time to prepare a properly structured Will. This is your final act. This is the document that instructs how to distribute all of the things you have worked so hard for during your life. You should make sure it is clear, concise, and properly drafted.

Seek the advice of a lawyer for this one. Yes, it is worth paying a professional to do this.

Life and Financial Goals

This section puts all your thoughts and dreams into a format that is tangible and useful. It helps you to see what your goals are, and whether they are achievable. It should list your goals as well as their associated costs and year of projected completion (see Chapter 2, Setting and Achieving Goals). This should clearly illustrate whether you can afford these goals, and how to achieve those that are possible. It may sometimes contain unpleasant results; for example, it may tell you that a particular goal is unaffordable unless your after-tax income increases by x number of dollars. **Life Goals Planning** gives you at least an idea of what goals are realistic and when they are achievable. This helps put many things in perspective, and can help you prioritize. It may be that you will have to give up buying that $15,000 boat in three years, but that may allow you to put in the swimming pool you always dreamed of having.

Cashflow Analysis (The Budget)

How you manage your monthly cashflow determines whether goals are met. A Cashflow Analysis is a key instrument; it can help establish a proper savings plan to assist you in reaching your objectives. This should include a detailed breakdown of your monthly income and expenditures, as well as suggestions on how to maximize your cashflow. Even individuals who earn $100,000 or more should have a monthly cashflow sheet (budget). Many times, it is these individuals who will benefit the most from it. Cashflow is where dreams are made. This is where you can set aside some money for that trek to the Himalayas in ten years, or for that six-week trip to China in five years. Taking the time to analyze your monthly cashflow in detail and then automating your monthly routine is a crucial step to reaching your dreams. More on this in the next chapter.

Action Plan

The action plan is usually a one-page document listing all the key steps required to accomplish your goals. When we conduct reviews with clients, we always refer back to this document prior to the meeting to ensure that, together, we have completed these steps or are in the process of completing them. Working with a Personal Finance Coach offers a certain level of accountability, and helps urge you to get things done. Have you ever flossed the night before a dental appointment because you want to make up for the last six months of not flossing? Same thing happens when you work with a PFC, a lot of to-dos get done right before annual reviews.

Plan Appendices

This is where you will find the nuts and bolts—the behind-the-scenes information about calculations and recommendations. For example, one appendix should include a detailed breakdown of your Net Worth. The Retirement Planning appendix will include your projected investment balances for each year going forward. At your regular reviews, this will allow you and your PFC to track your progress and see if your investments are on target. This is essential, as it helps keep you focused on your target, and not on the gyrations of the markets.

Personalizing Your Plan

Unfortunately, there is no cookie-cutter method to producing a proper, personalized financial plan. There is software that can produce a simple retirement projection in twenty minutes, but to truly complete a comprehensive and personalized plan takes a minimum of five to ten hours. Most plans, in fact, take well in excess of that to complete. One of the plans we developed for a doctor took over twenty-five hours to finalize, but the results were worth it. We were able to recommend savings of over $50,000 to the estate, plus $5,000 of annual tax savings. There was a fee for the plan, but the savings far outweighed the costs.

If your plan is not tailored to your life and your goals, then why have one at all? Don't take shortcuts in this department: spend the time it takes with a certified professional to come up with a comprehensive picture of where you're at and where you'd like to be headed in order to reach your goals.

Making the Plan Work

Your plan becomes your personal map for your journey towards many of your life and financial goals. There is comfort to be gained from knowing that all scenarios have been reviewed and planned for accordingly. This can give you the peace of mind to enjoy other things in life, such as quality time with your family or pursuing a hobby.

Remember, a plan is only as useful as what you do with it. If you had a plan prepared for you and you never reviewed it again, how would you know how you were doing? It is crucial to constantly update and evaluate your plan. I suggest annual or semi-annual reviews to have a firm handle on your financial picture. It is important that you have somebody else involved in the review process. This will ensure that many of the to-dos get done. Among many other things, your financial planner/advisor can act as your conscience as, without this motivating factor, your plan may become quickly out of date.

Chapter Summary

Your Financial Plan

Having a plan is your key to reaching your life goals. Work with a PFC (a financial planner/advisor) and don't put off creating a plan until it's too late: the sooner it's in place, the more income-earning years and time you will have to fulfill your goals.

A Map to the Future

Your plan should include:

- an Executive Summary
- a statement of your Net Worth
- your Retirement Plan, Portfolio Recommendations
- a strategy for Taxes, Insurance and your Estate
- your Life and Financial Goals
- a Cashflow Analysis and an Action Plan.

Personalizing Your Plan

The best-thought-out plans don't work unless they are uniquely tailored to your individual circumstances and take into account what you want to achieve.

Making the Plan Work

Annual or semi-annual reviews help to keep you on track, and ensure that you have a regular snapshot of your financial picture.

_____

CHAPTER
5

Getting the Most from Your Money

"I long to accomplish a great and noble task, but it is my chief duty to accomplish small tasks as if they were great and noble."
Helen Keller

The Envelope System

One of the most important aspects of the financial plan is the cashflow (budget) section. Cashflow is the heart of the financial plan. It determines how much money (blood flow) is pumped to which goal (organ). If you don't have a healthy heart, the rest of your organs and vital functions will suffer. Sometimes, the harmful effects aren't seen immediately, but show up as we age. The same applies to your finances. In an attempt to help you maximize your cashflow, I encourage automating regular transactions and using the envelope system.

Some people have an excellent handle on their monthly finances and may not need the envelope system or a modified version of it. But for those who need a straightforward way to get a handle on their monthly finances, this is for you.

The main premise of the envelope system is very simple: don't buy what you can't afford. As reasonable as this sounds, not many people follow this principle. We are bombarded by ads trumpeting "Buy Now, Pay Later"; "Don't Pay a Cent Event"; or "Refinance Your House For Next to Nothing!" It is not uncommon for people to borrow to buy big-screen TVs, computers or even cameras. The envelope system is a simple, proven method that allows people to live within their means while still doing the things they want to do.

It works like this: first, you list your household's monthly *net* (after tax and deductions) income. For example, if the amount you receive in your bank account from your employer every two weeks is $1,400, then your net monthly income is simply $2,800; don't worry about the extra two pays per year not being accounted for. Then you list your monthly expenses (see cashflow analysis worksheet on opposite page). Now that you have developed your list of goals, you will know many of the amounts required to achieve them.

You will find that many of your monthly expenses are relatively consistent and fixed, such as mortgage/rent, property taxes, utilities, retirement savings, goal savings, car loan/lease, etc. These fixed expenses should be automatically

Cashflow Analysis Worksheet

	Existing	Revised		
Pension Income (Net)	$_____	$_____		
Salary (Net)	$_____	$_____		
Spouse's Salary (Net)	$_____	$_____		
Other				
Monthly Net Income:	$_____	$_____		
Less:				
Mortgage/Rent	$_____	$_____		
House Insurance	$_____	$_____		
Property Taxes	$_____	$_____		
Car Loan	$_____	$_____		
Car Insurance	$_____	$_____		
Car Maintenance	$_____	$_____		
Pocket Money	$_____	$_____		
Other Loan	$_____	$_____		
Memberships	$_____	$_____		
Credit Card	$_____	$_____		
Groceries	$_____	$_____		
Utilities (cable, heat, hydro, phone, water)	$_____	$_____		
Clothing	$_____	$_____		
Entertainment	$_____	$_____		
Gifts	$_____	$_____		
Education Savings	$_____	$_____		
Travel	$_____	$_____		
Gas (automobile)	$_____	$_____		
Life Insurance	$_____	$_____		
House Maintenance	$_____	$_____		
Medical	$_____	$_____		
Charity	$_____	$_____		
Child Care	$_____	$_____		
Miscellaneous	$_____	$_____		
RRSP Savings	$_____	$_____		
Other Savings	$_____	$_____		
Large Trip/Emergency	$_____	$_____		
Other	$_____	$_____		
Other	$_____	$_____		
Total Expenses:	$_____	$_____		
Surplus / Shortfall	$_____	$_____		

debited from your bank account. This puts most of your monthly cashflow on automatic pilot.

Making Variable Expenses Fixed

Many of your more discretionary expenses, such as clothing, gifts, groceries, home maintenance, and entertainment are somewhat optional and vary every month; for example, gift expenses are usually much higher around the holidays. Start putting a fixed dollar amount to these discretionary expenses. Try and use a number that is realistic and that you would feel comfortable spending each month. For example, if you feel $300 per month is a reasonable amount to spend on entertainment, put that figure in the entertainment column. Do this with each category. When you get to the bottom of the list you should then add up all your expenses and deduct them from your net income. You should be running either a surplus (extra $$) or a shortfall (negative). If you are running a negative balance you should review and reduce where you can until you run a balanced budget. Remember, if you don't run a balanced budget each month, you will only continue to borrow to sustain the lifestyle you are living, and it will eventually catch up with you.

Implementing the System

Groceries are the one exception that cannot be radically reduced. They are not really optional, as we all need to eat on a regular basis. So, for groceries, if your monthly budget is $600, then I suggest that with each pay (assuming you are paid bi-weekly)

you take $300 cash (yes cash!) and place it in an envelope labelled Groceries. Use this cash to pay for your groceries.

Next up, set up envelopes for the other usual expenses. Label your envelopes as follows (dollar amounts are for you to fill in, these are just examples): Gifts ($200 per month), Clothing ($200

per month), Entertainment ($300 per month), Home Maintenance ($100 per month). You now know you have discretionary expenses of $800 per month, or $400 per pay. When you receive your pay, place $100 in the gift envelope, $100 in the clothing envelope, $150 in the entertainment envelope, and $50 in the home maintenance envelope.

Yes, it is a little cumbersome, but it works. And yes, you should physically put cash into the envelopes. Now what do you do? Anytime you want to do something under the Entertainment heading, such as order pizza delivery on Friday nights, use the cash in that envelope. If there is no cash in the Entertainment envelope, unfortunately, that means no pizza tonight—so get cooking! Conversely, if you haven't used any Entertainment money in four months, you would have $1,200 saved up. Reward yourself—perhaps go away for a golf weekend!

The Gift envelope will build, as this is a seasonal expense. Most of your spending will occur at certain times of the year, i.e. Christmas, birthdays, etc., so don't spend it on something else if you notice it's bulging with cash! Clothing is similar to Gifts: we don't usually spend on clothes on a regular basis. Again, only use cash from your Clothing envelope to buy clothes. If there is not enough money in the envelope to buy your outfit, then you'll have to wait. You could take some from your entertainment budget to afford it, but that would mean a sacrifice on the entertainment front. It's up to you. If you are uncomfortable with the idea of having cash on hand in the home, then you could set up a separate account and have the bi-weekly amount automatically go to this account. But then you would have to track how much of the balance in the account was for each expense, and this could prove quite time-consuming. Our clients have tried many methods, and the cash method seems to work best.

The Debt-Free Universe

The envelope system makes money real again. Credit cards, direct payment, cheques, buy now and pay later plans: money has become virtual, and it's very easy to lose track of something that was never physically in your hand to begin with. Our society is far too focused on having everything we need or want *now*, which is why we are the most indebted civilization in history. If you don't have the cash to buy it, the evident thing to do is to wait until you do. This was patently obvious to previous generations, but seems to be a new concept to people in their high-spending years today. And of course, there are whole industries that have a vested (and very profitable) interest in keeping you in debt. As the worlds of marketing, industry, and banking have become more sophisticated, they have managed to convince us that debt is the norm and not the exception.

Evidently, living debt-free cannot apply to all items, such as homes and cars, as they are generally too expensive to be able to buy cash-in-hand. This doesn't, however, extend to that new surround-sound system. You will notice that when you delay most purchases, it doesn't truly impact your life and you don't really miss the item in question.

Debt is the most influential factor stopping people from creating wealth and achieving their goals. If it is used without care, it will eventually catch up with you and cause your finances and possibly other areas of your life to collapse. I have seen several marriages end due to unwise borrowing. So it's back to the envelope system; it is the most effective method I have seen to allow people to live within their means while still saving towards their goals. Remember, this isn't a punishment. It's a way to control and maximize your monthly cashflow. Whether you earn $25,000 or $200,000 per year, you can apply the envelope system, or a modified version of it, to your lifestyle.

Real Families

One of my favourite clients regularly uses the envelope system to manage the family's monthly cashflow. Since implementing this method, this client has told me that he and his wife feel a sense of control over how and where their money is being spent. As a couple, they feel the money disagreements have all but disappeared, as they now live within the agreed-upon expense levels. For example, now his spouse knows she has $300 per month she can spend on home decorating without having to "get them approved." This client says they cannot imagine going back to the old way of doing things. By the way, this is a family that has a net worth of well over $1 million and earns an annual household income of over $170,000! So it works for all income brackets. Another family, a working couple with three children, resisted the envelope system for years. Then due to growing debt and a sense of being out of control, they decided to give the system a real try. Two years later, they are envelope-system believers. Their debts have been reduced dramatically, and they finally took that family vacation they had always dreamed of but were never able to afford.

This is not to say the first couple of months will not be challenging, but believe me, it is worth it. After four to five months it will become routine and, yes, you will be frustrated at times because you don't have the cash to buy something you really, really want. But sometimes that can be a good thing. It should eliminate spontaneous buying, and will allow you to appreciate the item even more when you do finally get it. It will also allow you to set aside money for your long-term goals and run a balanced budget. Those are truly satisfying achievements, and key steps in helping you to meet your life goals.

Chapter Summary

The Envelope System

Automate all your fixed expenses, and then determine how much discretionary income you have left and where you will spend it (i.e., clothing, entertainment). This practical exercise will allow you to balance your books—on paper, at least!

Implementing the System

Parcel out your surplus cash from every paycheque into separate envelopes for each category of spending. Do not spend any more than is in the envelope.

The Debt-Free Universe

Debt is almost a given in the modern world, but it is the single largest obstacle to achieving your personal and financial goals. Use common sense and the Envelope System to avoid this obstacle.

Real Families

Real people, from everyday families with modest incomes to retired millionaires, are using the Envelope System and living very comfortable lives. Furthermore, they have the peace of mind that comes from knowing exactly how much money they have to spend and where that money is going.

CHAPTER
6

Why You Need a Personal Finance Coach

---

*"Character is the real foundation
of all worthwhile success."*

John Hays Hammond

Making Your Decision

One of the most important decisions you will make regarding your finances is whether to enlist the services of a professional financial planner/advisor. Many people feel they do not need a planner/advisor and can manage on their own. This may be true for some individuals, but it is worth noting that all of the greatest athletes in the world have worked with a coach. Do you think Tiger Woods would be where he is today without the guidance of someone who knew the game, the discipline it required, and who also knew that keeping to a plan was the key to victory? Tiger got to live out his dream because he had (and still has) what is essential for a winning strategy: a great coach.

A good financial planner/advisor becomes a coach for your financial affairs, and, by coaching you, helps you to find the most efficient route to achieving your goals. Not only will your coach provide a map for reaching these goals, but, as with any athlete, will act as your conscience and help to keep you on track. The end result will ultimately be up to you, but it can help to know that there are checks and balances in your plan. For every great athlete there is a great coach, and the same should apply to you.

The Personal Finance Coach

What is a Personal Finance Coach (PFC)? A PFC is a unique type of financial planner/advisor. They will not go under the title of Personal Finance Coach; this is simply how they are referred to in this book.

They will meet with you, get to know you, and set you up with a comprehensive financial plan that helps you visualize the future. They will collect information to better understand your personal, financial and life goals. They will help manage your investments, your life goals, your cashflow and your retirement plans. A PFC is a professional who always has your best interest in mind. Every time I meet a prospective client, I ask them if I can review their existing financial plan. Nine times out of ten, there is no plan at all. A plan is not just recommendations on how to invest your portfolio; that is really only a small part of the plan. As discussed in Chapter 4 ("Your Roadmap to the Future"), a comprehensive financial plan should look at all aspects of one's finances, including life goals, cashflow, investing and, of course, retirement planning.

A PFC will take the time to get to know you and your personal risk tolerance, and then recommend investments that will help you achieve the lifestyle and retirement you want. The PFC is focused on the long term and on your Life Goals Plan.

I should mention my obvious bias. I am a financial planner and therefore, I usually suggest that people need a financial planner/advisor. However, I can tell you that this is not only based on my experience and a strong belief, but is also based on research. Studies suggest investors who use advisors do better than those who do not. A study by Boston-based Dalbar Financial Services, Inc. found that over a ten-year period, investors who worked with financial advisors outperformed no-load investors by 20% in equity mutual funds and by more than 17% in fixed income funds.

Why? One suggested reason was that investors who worked with financial advisors held their investments for longer periods of time, increasing their opportunities for growth. Aside from these investment benefits, there are many other aspects of having a Personal Finance Coach that can add to your bottom line, including tax, estate, mortgage and goal planning advice, which can save thousands of dollars. Finally, a PFC provides you with a fresh set of eyes on your financial picture, and will provide the framework you need to bring your life goals to fruition.

The Right Stuff

In our industry, there are many investment advisors and planners that focus almost exclusively on the investment aspect of finances and do not focus on financial planning. These advisors/planners are great if you are only looking for investment advice, however, you should know that these investment advisors/planners usually charge/earn the same as would a Personal Finance Coach who will look at all of your financial objectives including investments. It is for this reason that I am constantly surprised that individuals "settle" for simply investment advice (as good as it may be) because they believe it is less expensive than seeking the advice of a "true" financial planner. Many financial planners/advisors offer the full spectrum of services; take advantage of what is available to you. Make sure your planner/advisor is adding value to your financial picture.

As with all professions, there is a range of quality of service among financial planners/advisors, and it is your task to ask the right questions in order to find someone who is suitable for you and your needs.

In most households, there is usually one individual who handles the family finances. Imagine if this person were to pass on, you would want someone trustworthy, competent and caring to assist the remaining family members with their financial affairs. When you meet someone who you feel would fill that role, you have found your PFC.

The Advisory Team

Ultimately, you should have a PFC who is competent, and whom you like and trust. Alongside this Personal Finance Coach, you will need an advisory team consisting of an accountant, a lawyer and various other professionals to suit your circumstances. A PFC has developed your plan, and is therefore in a position to advise you where and when you need these professionals, and for what actions and strategies. In most cases, a PFC can recommend individuals whom they've worked with before and whom they trust will do a good job.

While some forgo the added expense of enlisting the experts, I believe that many need a competent accountant to help with complex tax scenarios. It is also extremely helpful to enlist the services of a lawyer who specializes in real estate and one who specializes in estate planning. The Personal Finance Coach then acts as the quarterback to your advisory team seeking out these professionals to implement some of the recommended strategies. Remember, many of the strategies are designed to save you or your beneficiaries money.

The Quest for Trust: Choosing the Right Personal Finance Coach

You will know you have found the right PFC when you meet him or her. As with the people you meet in your life, both on a personal and business level, you and your prospective PFC either "click" or you don't. Follow your gut in this department. Beyond first impressions, you should feel a sense of trust and be able to understand their planning and investment philosophy.

10 key questions to ask your potential PFC are:

1. **How long have you been in the financial services industry?** (As with many professionals, experience can be very beneficial. Advisors with five or more years of experience are preferred.)

2. **What level of service can I expect?** Will I be dealing with you directly, or a member of your team?

3. **What is your investment philosophy?** (If they don't have an immediate answer, get up and run—don't walk—away.)

4. **How many clients do you have?** (An advisor with too many clients may not be able to provide the level of service you require. Typically, any more than 350 households may be too many.)

5. **Do you have any professional qualifications, such as the Certified Financial Planner designation?**

6. **How often will we meet to review my plan?** (You should meet semi-annually or annually.)

7. **How are you compensated?** (A good PFC should be straightforward in his/her response.)

8. **Will I receive a financial plan?** If so, what does it contain? May I see a sample plan?

9. **How much will my financial plan cost?** (Beware of the "free" financial plans. There may be strings attached or it may not be a comprehensive or personalized plan.)

10. **What information will you need from me?** (Will they review your tax and estate planning information? The more information they review, the more comprehensive the plan.)

Remember, you need to find a PFC whom you can trust. If you constantly suspect that their recommendations are best suited to their pocketbook, rather than your needs, then you probably want to change planners/advisors.

How to Find a Personal Finance Coach

The best way to find a Personal Finance Coach is through referrals from colleagues, family or friends. Most successful financial planners/advisors (PFCs) do not advertise, as most of their business is derived from referrals. If the referral route doesn't work for you, then look in your local Yellow Pages or online for financial planners/advisors in your community.

When you interview a potential advisor, ask for an information package, or visit their Website to learn more about them and what types of services they offer. You should focus on those that offer comprehensive financial planning. See if he/she is a Certified Financial Planner (CFP). CFPs have a code of ethics and practice standards that they must adhere to. This requires them to offer a certain level of financial planning, which, in theory, should include a personalized financial plan that suits your resources and needs. Unfortunately, the CFP designation does not ensure that you will receive a full financial plan, as some CFPs do not provide this service. So it is crucial to be thorough and ask as many questions as possible.

When interviewing potential PFCs you should be aware that many will also be interviewing you, as they want to ensure that you fit their practice in terms of personality and expectations. Remember, this is a two-way relationship and hopefully a long-term one. Nobody benefits if it isn't a good fit.

When looking for a Personal Finance Coach, take your time; don't choose one until you've reviewed the financial plan; and only if it all makes sense and feels right should you proceed. PFCs are looking for long-term relationships and want you to be very comfortable and confident with your decision.

Where Dreams Become Action Plans

I find my line of work extraordinarily rewarding, because I get to see the natural progression from thought to paper to reality. In some cases, our clients include all living generations of the family: grandparents, parents and children. Each element of the family has a different planning need, but each has a large impact on the other. We plan accordingly to assist all three generations to achieve their goals and dreams. It is wonderful to watch families achieve balance, serenity and excitement towards life. It's one of the most gratifying feelings I have experienced.

I cannot stress enough how important a Personal Finance Coach is to the achievement of your life and financial goals. Find the person who is right for you and begin to turn your dreams into action plans today.

Chapter Summary

Making Your Decision

Do you use an advisor or go it alone? A financial advisor will act as a coach, helping you to craft a solid and realistic plan, and will periodically review that plan so that you stick to it.

The Personal Finance Coach

A PFC will take the time to get to know you and your personal circumstances, and will look at all of your financial objectives, including investments.

The Advisory Team

The Personal Finance Coach helps you to select outside professionals to offer advice on your plan, and then quarterbacks this advisory team. A team is most often comprised of an accountant and one or more lawyers.

The Quest for Trust: Choosing the Right Advisor

You need to choose a PFC with whom you feel comfortable. Ask the 10 Key Questions to verify that this PFC is right for you.

How to Find a Personal Finance Coach

Referrals are the most common means of finding a PFC. Interview your PFC to find out if their investment and planning philosophy meshes with your own.

Where Dreams Become Action Plans

Find a coach who will work for your best interests in crafting this plan.

_____

CHAPTER
7

Value Your Money

*"I can't understand it. I can't even understand
the people who can understand it."*
Queen Juliana of the Netherlands

O nce you have chosen your PFC, it is essential to find
the right investment mix to enable you to achieve all
the items on your list of goals. Of course, the very
reason you've chosen to work with a Personal Finance Coach
in the first place is that they can offer advice in this area. A
tangible action plan begins with questions: this is where you
go back to your personal and financial goals. When do you
want to retire? What dreams would you like to achieve in the
next five years? The next ten years? The next twenty? The
answers to these questions will dictate whether you choose a
riskier investment with higher possible returns, or a more
secure investment that will pay out lower returns. Follow these
7 Steps to Successful Investing:

1. Understand Your Investments

Ask questions. Before you ever invest in anything, it is crucial that you understand what it is you are investing in and the risks involved. Many people will throw thousands of dollars at a hot stock tip without even thinking twice about it, but when it comes to buying a computer or a TV, they will shop around for days for the right features and price. A lot of people who bought Nortel were driven by emotion (greed) and had no idea what product Nortel actually produced. The same is true for hot tips or "sure" things. The saying "Buyer beware" should always be at the forefront of your mind for any type of purchase, and that includes investments.

Not understanding your investments, which often goes hand-in-hand with emotional investing, will bring with it great anxiety when things start heading south. I usually compare this to my fear of flying. To most people, especially pilots, flying is not an emotional experience. It is simply a way to get from point A to point B. Well, not for me: it is a terrifying experience. I find it incomprehensible how a plane can actually remain in flight. When we hit turbulence, I scream to my wife "we're going down." Every time, she calmly assures me that turbulence is normal and everything will be fine and we will get to Point B safely.

The same fears apply to investing. If you don't understand the nature of the market or the investment you have chosen, of course it becomes scary when we begin to experience market turbulence. However, market turbulence is part of the territory. Most investments will have ups and downs. Depending on the vehicle, some of these highs will be very high, and some of the lows can be very low.

There are numerous books that describe the different types of investments that exist and their associated benefits and risks. I have purposely only touched on this topic, as I believe the other books have covered this subject with sufficient detail. Again, you can spend your time exhaustively researching the subject, or you can hire a PFC who does this for a living and can explain it to you clearly and concisely.

If you take the time to understand what you are investing in, these highs and lows will be an expected part of the game. By the same token, if I took the time to learn how a plane worked, I can guarantee that my fear of flying would disappear. There will always be turbulence in investing; it's just the nature of the beast. Just remember to stay seated, keep your seatbelt fastened, and make sure you have a competent pilot flying your plane.

2. Don't Overanalyze

Don't fall into the trap of checking the value of your investments daily. This is simply a waste of time. If you are invested for the long term, the daily fluctuations of the markets mean little to your plan. This could be likened to checking your cholesterol level daily if you have a cholesterol problem. Nobody does that; why do it with your investments? A well-crafted portfolio should do quite well over the long term. Remember, long term means seven years and longer, not two or three years.

I recommend looking at your portfolio quarterly and doing a full review annually with your advisor. Remember, you are paying your advisor to assist and advise you so that you can redirect your precious time to the more enjoyable things in life.

3. Don't Follow the Pack

Let's say you've found a PFC you are happy with, and have become comfortable reviewing your investments quarterly (rather than daily). The next step is to turn a blind eye to the hype: it is virtually guaranteed that friends, colleagues, the media, and yes, even your own family will have opinions on where the market is headed and what the hot investments are. It's very easy to get caught up in this and take it out on your portfolio. The dot-com phenomenon and subsequent crash should have taught us our lesson in this department, but everyone continues to be eager to be on the ground floor of the "next big thing."

Your PFC will, of course, have recommendations of his or her own, and your annual review is the time to evaluate this information and decide what to do with it. In most cases, this means staying the course.

4. Buy Quality

When investing in mutual funds, review the funds' holdings. Do you recognize some of the company names? Are these well-known companies with a strong brand name? Invest in companies that have a proven record and can withstand a market downturn, which in turn protects your capital. Your PFC can walk you through the different investment holdings.

5. Stay the Course

If you understand your investments and have put together an action plan to meet your goals, don't panic when your investments drop. Always remember that your investments were selected to allow you to achieve your personal goals with time horizons taken into account.

As an investor, it is important to know that typically the stock market may drop up to 10% in any given year. And every five years the market may drop up to 20%. With all the volatility you may ask, why even invest in the stock market? Well, on the positive side, over the long term there are very few investments that have performed as well as stocks [represented by the two Standard & Poor (S&P) stock indices below]. See chart A below which compares stock performance to that of a guaranteed investment certificate (GIC).

CHART A   **Stocks vs. GICs**

	5 year	10 year	20 year
S&P 500 Total Return Index in CDN $	-6.0%	8.7%	11.7%
S&P/TSX Composite Total Return Index	1.1%	10.0%	9.3%
5 Year Guaranteed Investment Certificates (GIC)	3.7%	4.5%	6.9%

Source: Andex Associates Inc., Compound Annual Returns as of June 30, 2005

Keep in mind that even a difference of a couple of percentage points makes a huge difference in the future value of your investment. Chart B illustrates how a $100 invested in each of the following investments would have grown from 1950 to June 30, 2005.

CHART B   Growth of a $100 Investment

	1950	June 30, 2005	% return
S&P 500 Total Return Index in CDN $	$100	$60,668	12.2%
S&P/TSX Composite Total Return Index	$100	$25,743	10.5%
5 Year Guaranteed Investment Certificates (GIC)	$100	$5,098	7.3%

Source: Andex Associates Inc.

As you can see, owning stocks has proven to be quite rewarding over the long term. As well, if your plan requires that you earn 8%, it will be difficult to achieve this without owning any stocks in your portfolio. As veteran financial advisor and finance author, Nick Murray, once said, "I don't know which way the next ten percent, or even twenty percent, move in the market will be. I know exactly in which direction the next hundred percent move will be, and that's what I'm investing for."

6. Pay Yourself First

Pay yourself first simply means making automatic contributions directly into your retirement or investment account. This painless approach has proven to be one of the most successful methods of accumulating savings. Think of it like you would a mortgage payment, it just becomes one of your monthly expenses. After a couple of years you will not believe how much you were able to save.

7. Focus on the Long Term

As we've discussed in earlier chapters, the whole idea of having a financial plan is to allow you to enjoy yourself today while planning for tomorrow. You and your Personal Finance Coach will be earmarking funds towards your successive goals; after all, the reason you've undertaken this journey is to enjoy life and to actually achieve the items on your list. But there is a fine line between reasonable expenditure now and blowing the budget for later plans. Your principle financial concern should be to provide a comfortable retirement, and that means planning for the long term while fulfilling affordable goals along the way.

The investments that will take you there are not generally the flashy variety, but rather offer slow, dependable growth. Your PFC will advise you if any changes need to be made to your portfolio as time goes by.

Chapter Summary

Understand Your Investments

Educating yourself is the key to avoiding the pitfalls of the marketplace. Your PFC should be able to help you understand different investment vehicles and select the ones that are right for you.

Don't Overanalyze

Once you and your PFC have selected the makeup of your portfolio, don't waste your time checking on the markets and analyzing the results. Highs and lows in the markets are normal.

Don't Follow the Pack

The hype that surrounds the hot investments of the day rarely pays off. Keep to your plan and watch your money grow, not over days or months, but over years.

Buy Quality

Invest in companies that have a proven record and can withstand a market downturn.

Stay the Course

Patience with your investments and reviewing them regularly with your PFC is the surest route to success.

Pay Yourself First

Begin an automatic contribution program directly into your retirement or investment account.

Focus on the Long Term

The cornerstone of your plan should be to provide a comfortable retirement, and as such, the investments that will take you there; focus on long-term growth.

CONCLUSION

Something's Gotta Give

"Twenty years from now you will be more disappointed by the things you didn't do than by the things you did."

Mark Twain

Think back on all the years that you have been working. Add up how much you have earned and then how much you have saved. Do the same exercise for your Life Goals. How many goals have you had that are unfulfilled? The results may be shocking! If you don't want to be as shocked ten years from now, you have to make a significant change in the way you plan, save and spend.

Let's use an example of someone aged forty-five, who has been working for twenty years and has averaged $50,000 annually in earnings. That would mean they have earned one million dollars during their career. Chances are, their net worth is $100,000 or less. Consider that this individual has only fifteen to twenty years left to work, or roughly the same amount of time as they have already worked. If they continue as they have for the past twenty years, they will likely not have anywhere near enough for a proper retirement or for meeting many of their life goals.

I challenge you to try the exercises described in previous chapters—yes, even including the envelope system. You will be pleasantly surprised by the results.

Schedule Some Time for the Good Life

Why not block off an hour a week to just sit with your family (or on your own) and see how you are progressing towards your life and financial goals. Try and envision how great it will feel when you achieve some of your goals. It's important to spend a little time each week refocusing on you and your goals so they do not get lost in the clutter and speed of life. Make sure that you also schedule time to actually perform these goals.

Let's Get to It

As for finding a PFC and having a plan developed, I encourage you to do this immediately. Maybe you are already dealing with a PFC. Ask your existing planner/advisor if they would be willing to assist you with many of the topics discussed. If they do not offer these services, challenge them to do so. Your dreams and goals rely on their guidance and assistance. But if they just don't offer **Life Goals Planning**, then you may wish to consider finding someone in your area who does.

Congratulations on having come this far on the road to achieving the goals and dreams you have for yourself and your family. Now that you have read the book, it's time to put your thoughts, dreams and goals into action. Remember, once a goal or a thought is put on paper, it becomes a more tangible reality.

I wish you the best of luck with your adventure. I hope it brings you all the security, comfort, love, freedom and self-actualization that you desire. Most importantly, I wish you *no regrets* in life.

Your 10-Week Action Plan

"Come on, vámonos.
Everybody let's go.
Come on, let's get to it.
I know that we can do it."

Dora the Explorer™, Nick Jr (Nickelodeon)

A Call to Action: Build the Plan

You're at the end of the book—what will you do now? Here is a 10-week action plan to help you turn your goals into reality.

Week 1: Set your Goals

Try to think big, but also think realistically. If a plan is set up with unrealistic goals, it will almost surely disappoint.

Weeks 2-3: Find Your Personal Finance Coach

If you are not receiving the type of planning services that you want, look for somebody who offers these services. If you are pleased with your existing planner/advisor but they do not offer these services, ask them if they can. If not, let the hunt begin.

Call associations to find a Certified Financial Planner in your area. *CFP is the only internationally recognized designation for financial planning. To find a list of CFPs in your area, contact the Financial Planners Standards Council of Canada at Tel: 416.593.8587. Toll Free: 1.800.305.9886 or http://www.cfp-ca.org*

Your objective is to interview approximately three different financial planners/advisors. Try to find out if what they have to offer matches what you are looking for.

Be sure to ask to see a sample financial plan. This will tell you what type of detail and planning they offer. Make sure it includes cashflow planning (budgeting). This is crucial to your chances of achieving your goals and enjoying life now while planning for tomorrow.

- Ask how many hours it takes them to prepare a plan.
- Ask if they can implement the plan for you as well.
- Ask for testimonials. Visit their website or request an information package to learn more.

Remember to ask the 10 key Questions, found in Chapter 6.

Weeks 3-4: Make a Decision

Decide which advisor you would like to prepare your financial plan. Do not procrastinate—send them the required documents to begin your plan immediately. Your plan should be completed within two to three weeks. (It should be complete by week 7 or 8.) Don't just select the plan that is the least costly or free; chances are, this will not be a full financial plan but more of an investment proposal, or it will be a standard, boilerplate plan that can be completed in under an hour. These plans are not personalized, and can be confusing and hard to implement. You are looking for a plan with an executive summary detailing your situation and what needs to be done. It should also include a list of steps required to implement the plan.

Weeks 5-8: Educate Yourself

Read at least two books on investing and/or financial planning. My favourites are:

Simple Wealth, Inevitable Wealth by Nick Murray. This is an excellent book on the merits of long term investing and why stocks can be so helpful in reaching our goals.

The Wealthy Barber by David Chilton. This Canadian classic teaches the basics of financial planning through conversations with Roy the barber and his customers.

Week 8-10: Review Your Plan

Now all your hard work should begin paying off. Take a good look at your new plan; make sure it encompasses all of your goals and objectives. Review which goals are feasible and which are unattainable. Make minor modifications to the plan if required. Review the cashflow section to make sure that it can be implemented and that you understand it.

Week 10 and On: Implement and Monitor the Plan

If you are comfortable with the plan and with your PFC, call your PFC and begin implementing the plan. Don't forget the envelope system. Make sure you meet with your advisor annually or semi-annually to ensure the plan is being followed and is on target. Make certain the steps to implementing the plan are being completed as per the plan projection. Remember, a great plan is of no use if it sits in a file gathering dust. Add life goals as they arise and discuss with your PFC how to attain them.

NOTES

Chilton, David. *The Wealthy Barber*. Prima Lifestyles Publishing, 1991.

DALBAR Financial Services, Inc., study between 1984 and 1993, citing FundRATE. Returns do not take into consideration any sales charge or fees. The investment results represent past performance, which is no guarantee of future results.

Danko, William D., and Stanley, Thomas J. *The Millionaire Next Door*. Longstreet Press, 1996.

Loomis, Carol J. "Warren Buffett Gives Away His Fortune." *Fortune*. June 25, 2006. <http://money.cnn.com/w006/06/25/magazines/fortune/charity1.fortune/index.htm>

Maslow, Abraham. "A Theory of Human Motivation." *Psychological Review* 50:370-396, 1943.

Murray, Nick. *Simple Wealth, Inevitable Wealth*. The Nick Murray Company, Inc, 1999.

Some elements of the *5 Biggest Mistakes People Make with Money* were inspired by an unknown source.

ABOUT THE AUTHOR

Robert Abboud is the President and founder of Wealth Strategies, Investment and Financial Planning, a fee-based financial planning firm located in Ottawa. He has worked in the financial services industry since 1991, has a Bachelor of Economics from Ottawa University, and holds both the Personal Financial Planner (PFP) designation issued by the Institute of Canadian Bankers as well as the Certified Financial Planner (CFP) designation issued by the Financial Planners Standards Council (FPSC) of Canada.

Rob left his position at the bank after five years and decided to establish Wealth Strategies in 1996. He wanted to create a unique financial planning practice that focused on assisting a very select clientele. Rob is involved in helping his clients not only plan for the future, but also achieve life goals along the way. As Rob's practice is near capacity, he felt he could help a larger group of individuals by sharing his thoughts on life goals planning through this book.

A recipient of the Ottawa Business Journal's prestigious Forty under 40 award and the Queens Golden Jubilee Commemorative Medal, Rob has always been an active member of his local community.

Rob lives in Ottawa with his wife Brigitte and his son Jeremy.

For more information on this book please visit www.lifegoalsplanning.com

NO
REGRETS

Finding The Right Path With A Personal Finance Coach

A Common Sense Guide to *Achieving* and *Affording* Your Life Goals

For copies of this book visit
www.lifegoalsplanning.com
or if you have any questions please contact
us at info@lifegoalsplanning.com